THE ART OF PROFESSIONAL PROSPECT

A PROFESSIONAL SALES LEADER'S HANDBOOK
FOR CAREER SUCCESS

BY BURT VILLARREAL

The Art of Professional Prospecting ©2012 by Burt Villarreal
First Revision, 2012
Second Revision, 2019
Third Revision, 2023

Printed in the United States of America

Cover and book design by:
Rebecca DeNeau
Eric Collander
becreative.designlab@gmail.com

Edited by BAABCO Leadership Consulting

ISBN: 9780934955980

Published by Watercress Press
15083 Spring Mist
San Antonio, TX 78247
www.watercresspress.com

McDonald's, Apple, USANA, LinkedIn, Google. Jason's Deli and Jimmy Johns are national/global companies and are mentioned only for illustration purposes.

Sales Force, Sales Chain, Monday.com, Microsoft Outlook, Paul Martinelli are specific products or industry leaders and are mentioned as tools and resources to further the purposes of this book.

Dedication

To my wife Alicia; without her great love and coaching I could not have realized this journey.

To our children; we are blessed to be their parents and are confident that God continues to have great things in store for them.

To my mother and father; together they gave me confidence, wisdom, love, perseverance, and appreciation.

Foreword

I began writing the *Art of Professional Prospecting (AOPP)* early in my sales career. The purpose was to help all Sales Professionals and Leaders, including myself, surpass the competition, especially by focusing on what is the first and often overlooked component of successful territory management and sales:

Daily Net New Prospecting.

Too often, even the best professionals are led off track by their own excuses and do not persevere with Daily Net New Prospecting. The results are often inconsistent monthly production or worse; failure to achieve the ultimate objective: meeting and exceeding their annual quota. In other words, having a weak Sales Pipeline strategy.

The AOPP will help you plan, prepare, and execute your strategy in order to adequately balance the Daily Net New Prospecting, which, in conjunction with the necessary follow-up calls, is the winning combination needed to develop more suspects than with the standard prospect mentality. The AOPP will also educate you on deploying my Ten By Ten Daily Net New Prospecting Strategy step by step, with very quick and successful results. It will define the many benefits of envisioning Suspects vs. Prospects and how to strategize with each, in relation to the expansion of your 30-day Pipeline.

Before I equip you to go to Daily War in your franchise, let us be certain that we are on the same definition of the Sales Pipeline. I define the Sales Pipeline as the preferred model of choice used by Professional Sales Leaders to manage individual short-mid and, long term sales opportunities. This Pipeline must be routinely reviewed and tested individually or with your leadership if you are part of a Sales Team. In addition, be aware that your Pipeline commitment quickly makes its path to the highest levels of senior management in your organization. Your Pipeline, accompanied with those of your fellow professionals, plays a major role in how the entire organization projects and manages revenues, expenses, budgets, compensation, inventory, hiring of personnel, and the return of investments back into the organization. This is critical in order to achieve profitable sustainability in their competitive market arenas.

Your 30-Day Pipeline should contain sufficient amounts of opportunities that take into consideration possible time delays, ultimately lifeless or lost sales, as well as those projected for certain sales success. In other words, Leader, you are not likely to win every opportunity every time. Upon review, within thirty days, your performance should demonstrate the results of Daily Net

New Prospecting and the consistent building of future opportunities, otherwise known as the 60 and 90 day Pipelines. Depending on the metrics for success utilized in your particular industry, you will then be well on your way to consistently meet or exceed quota, which will directly impact in return, your personal success. *Make Sense?*

Leader, over my successful sales career I have witnessed the tragedy of great closers consistently at 75% of quota alongside the glorious average closers who achieve over 100% of quota and consistently, *catch the competition asleep at the wheel*.

The difference in their performances is found in their Pipelines. One is solid while the other is hollow. The end results are due to the fact that, greater success in sales is built primarily from properly executing a balance of Daily Net New Prospecting with average closing talent, and not great closing talent combined with limited Net New Prospecting. Keep in mind, sales representatives are rarely dismissed because of incompetency. They are most often dismissed for lack of production. Look around your office. You will quickly observe that I am correct. Leader, at month end, it is not about being outsold by the competition. *It is about being out prospected!*

Before we grow further, here are a few fun facts!

FUN FACTS

"Pipeline"
appears **10** times in the book forward and **18** times throughout the rest of the book.

What message does that drive with you?

"Today" and "right now"
appear in **14** of the **22** Mental Workout questions.

How will that transform your daily action steps starting tomorrow?

Sales Professional, the primary message in the *Art of Professional Prospecting* is to drive daily net new prospecting, timely actions and ultimately, your high-level success.

Are you with me?

Preface

The Art of Professional Prospecting is my personal doctrine for new, seasoned, and senior Sales Professionals. It will deliver success strategies, based upon my best personal practices for a healthy Sales Pipeline, resulting from over 30 years of building highly successful and profitable territories (franchises).

If your assignment is to grow, maintain and profitably defend a territory or business, I trust you will include this guidebook in your personal arsenal of Sales War Tactics.

In addition, be certain to log into the BAABCO Sales Development App or BAABCO.biz. In the app you will find over 150 strategy questions and to-the-point answers to guide you from beginning to end in all of your successful sales initiatives and results.

Throughout *The Art of Professional Prospecting* guidebook, you will notice the BAABCO.biz links. The links are intended to direct you to the site, where you may find additional strategies to the subject content, including the BAABCO Sales Development App.
.

Essential Links for your success!

BAABCO Sales Development App
BAABCO.biz
BAABCO.biz/graph
BAABCO.biz/ten-by-ten
BAABCO.biz/7-components
BAABCO.biz/warrior-assessment

Books can be ordered from BAABCO.biz.

Contents

PROFIT POINTERS

IT'S SIMPLE ARITHMETIC:
YOUR INCOME CAN GROW
ONLY TO THE EXTENT THAT
YOU DO.

—*T. Harv Eker*

Growing Your Income
Advertising in Your Territory

Let's face it; unless you have the unique product that does it all, you will be up against tough competition. It comes in all forms: feature rich, name brand, lowest priced, or best value. This list goes on as far as the enumeration of different reasons why a Professional Sales Leader ever missed turning a prospect (suspect preferred) into a client.

One effective method to overcome the high hurdles of a cutthroat or even the most legitimate of your competitors, is to be there at the right time and with the right perceived value. However, even more critical to your success is the solid 30, 60, 90 Day Pipeline.

The right time has more than one significance: it means more than being there just for the close. It is being there early enough to know when the time is really right to begin educating your prospect (suspect preferred) toward the differences in your products, solutions, organization, and more importantly, YOU. In other words, *Your Four Corners!* (Paul Martinelli). This, is achieved and leads to the most effective results only through the daily prospecting of your territory. There are many ways in which you might approach it. Personally, you might define the strategy as cold calling, canvassing, networking, telemarketing, NBD, advertising in person or even blitzing.

There are too many of your competitors **SHOUTING IT OUT** in your territory and earning the respect and future business of the suspect/prospect who could very well become *your* client. You could literally have the answer to all the questions, yet it won't do your career any good unless you are willing to **SHOUT IT OUT.** The person who feels they can become a top performer without nurturing the prospect's trust does not deserve to reap the benefits that a consistent Net New Prospector earns. And don't think the call-ins of an established territory will do it for you. You are not the only one who owns a website, app, appears on Google searches, networks on LinkedIn, TikTok or Facebook. And if you are, you won't be for long. Speaking for myself, I have closed more prospects when I approached them first than when they called me first. I am referring specifically to the "call in" we tend to get too excited about, which often has served only to inform me that I would have to wait my turn to show our products. The prospect will be more loyal to you if you find them first. You then initiate and develop the suspect into a loyal prospect by establishing, building & maintaining rapport, as their trusted advisor.

Prospect (Suspect Preferred) defined:

I define a suspect as someone who has not yet realized that they are a prospect, your prospect, or your next client. Therefore, you have a greater opportunity to create interest, high value, need, desire and a sense of urgency. You are also more likely to eliminate some, or all of the competition in the sales process, you aim to control.

A prospect may already know their own intentions and has (very possibly) been educated by your competitor, who came before you. Additionally, you are likely to be stepping into a **PRICE WAR** if your product is viewed by many as a commodity.

REALITY POINT

I created and developed the Ten By Ten Daily Net New Prospecting Strategy more than 25 years ago. I recognized this critical need in order to improve my personal monthly sales results. *The fundamental strategy of the Ten By Ten is to change routine habits of task management between 8:30 to 10:00 a.m., which often derail us from the proper balance required to pursue Net New Prospecting.*

NOTES • IDEAS • INSPIRATION

_____

_____

_____

_____

_____

_____

_____

_____

MENTAL WORKOUT QUESTIONS:

1. What can I do differently today to begin generating more suspects from prospects?

_____

_____

_____

_____

2. How can I differentiate myself from my competitors when approaching those suspects?

_____

_____

_____

_____

SIX-MONTH REVISIT:

How would you answer Questions #1 and #2 above differently today?

1. _____

_____

_____

2. _____

_____

_____

IF YOU FOCUS ON GOALS,
YOU MAY HIT GOALS — BUT
**THAT DOESN'T GUARANTEE
GROWTH**. IF YOU FOCUS ON
GROWTH, YOU WILL GROW
AND ALWAYS HIT GOALS.

—*John C. Maxwell*

Identifying Personal Targets
Setting SMART Growth Goals

Now, that's a familiar phrase. However, make no mistake, it is a critical and fundamental component to the success of a Professional Sales Leader. Here is a simple formula that will help you to realize your goals a lot quicker and with more consistency:

Set your goals in writing. They must be:

Specific,
Measurable,
Attainable,
Relevant, and
Timebound

- Envision each growth goal with crystal clear vision.
- Carry and monitor your goals at least once per week.
- I do not recommend more than five to seven clear goals.

In summary, itemize the means by which you intend to achieve your growth goals. Monitor your progress regularly to see how you are progressing. Being vigilant will help you stay ahead of the situation in case you have slacked off or temporarily stalled. Be reasonable with yourself. If you aim too high or too quickly, you could become discouraged. That will not only impact a particular goal, but your motivation when it comes to setting future goals.

Know the metrics for your industry. The formulas (prospecting to appointments to close) for determining a six - figure income in your business may be different from those utilized by others. If you are not aware of them, find out immediately. It is difficult to set and achieve growth goals (that target more production and income) if you cannot properly forecast incoming sales transactions.

Obtain a picture of your goal if possible. Post it where it can be seen often to motivate you, perhaps on your desk, on your phone, on your nightstand or the mirror in your bathroom. I confess, I tried on each of my Rolexes at least five times before I purchased them.

You may wish to test drive your Mercedes, Jaguar, BMW, Bentley, Tesla, Maserati or Corvette. You may even take a tour of that ocean-front mansion. *Leader*, your goals may be unique, yet the formulas required to achieve them should be simple, truthful, and attainable.

REALITY POINT

I purchased a new Mercedes S550 a few years ago. I have always been a visionary. I am consistent and methodical in setting my growth goals. I set my eyes on the target, pursue it Quietly and with Heat-Seeking Missile Intensity.

NOTES • IDEAS • INSPIRATION

MENTAL WORKOUT QUESTIONS:

1. What professional and personal goals have I identified that I will pursue with Heat-Seeking Missile Intensity?

_____

_____

_____

_____

2. What will I do before the end of this day to ensure My Direct Impact?

_____

_____

_____

_____

SIX-MONTH REVISIT:

How would you answer Questions #1 and #2 above differently today?

1. _____

_____

_____

2. _____

_____

_____

PLAN FOR NEXT WEEK TODAY

AND NOT TODAY FOR TODAY — OR TOMORROW.

—*Burt Villarreal*

Quiet Before the Storm
Positive and Negative Motivation

What makes you *get up and go?* What makes you literally get up and make your growth goals your reality? This is a force that can only come from within you. You can feel it pounding in your heart. It almost pops out of your head, propelling you forward! You can be taught every selling technique ever formulated, but it won't result in triumph without positive motivation. You have to teach that skill set to yourself, or at least consent to be observant to the examples of others that surround you. Yes, *enthusiasm* can be contagious if you allow it to be.

Positive Motivation: It is created in you and you cannot receive it as a free gift. You have to chase it and you cannot purchase it. Top Sales Leaders, miracle physicians, winning attorneys, triumphant politicians, not to mention corporations such as McDonald's, Apple, USANA, just to name a few, all share this ultimate force. A consistent energy level is maintained and they never rest, even when they are leading the competition. Motivation is a nuclear bomb. It can serve the most positive purpose or it can lead to a total disaster if this tremendous force is used in a negative manner.

Negative Motivation: It exists. It has been called procrastination, laziness, personal problems, or busyness. However, rarely is it called by its actual name: **FEAR**. We all have experienced it at one time or another. I mention it because it is important and, to deconstruct it. Next time you are too tired, too busy, or procrastinating the situation ask yourself this: Is it really the force of negative motivation? If you admit to yourself that it is, you are officially halfway to zero. Now, simply turn this self-assessment into an opportunity, and transform it into your positive motivation. You *will* have a better day. Sales Leader, it is critical to our success that we recognize, own our present circumstances, and be willing to deconstruct them.

That first day, when you manage to defeat your **FEAR**, you will meet new suspects and prospects and when met with new objections, you will turn them into new opportunities. You will share your obstacles and victories with your family, friends and business associates. You will be busier than you have ever imagined, and you will have more opportunities available to you to secure the ultimate growth goals you have set for yourself. You owe it to yourself now more than ever before. *Am I right?* So, Leader, get up and out of the office right now! Get off social media or the internet. Stop using up the air conditioning, stop drinking the coffee, and start striving for a new level of personal excellence!

Need positive motivation from Burt?

FASTEN YOUR SEATBELT, HERE WE GO!

- Embrace the concept of Burt's Ten By Ten Daily Net New Prospecting calls from 8:30-10:00 a.m. Net New calls include anyone you have not contacted within 90 days; present, past or future clients.

- Fall in love with your sales career again (if needed) or risk losing it to someone else.

- Be the first or second prospector today in your franchise and not the eighth or tenth.

- Treat every day with urgency and as if it were the last closing day of the month: A *profitable* lesson to me from Dad.

- Avoid falling victim to an *unbalanced* amount of follow-up calls vs. net new.

- Think bigger and beyond yourself. Find a charitable organization that can depend on you monthly and unconditionally.

- Think beyond your present good health or financial condition; prepare well for your prosperous future.

- Build the courage (Pipeline) to fire a prospect if needed. This is easily attainable! *Raise* your Self Expectations!

- Know your industry metrics for success and get *very* excited about deploying your strategy.

- Be truthful about where you stand on those metrics and confirm your new growth strategy timeline with yourself and management if needed.

- Now, move or lose. A hungry Warrior is waiting to take your position if you fail. Sales do not lie. You either win or lose!

- Regain confidence in your company and products to inspire it in the eyes of new suspects. Know & sell on your unique values.

- Admit that the business is out there to earn, and take it from your competitors. *Are you earning your claim?*

- **My favorite:** Get excited about the competitors you will, "Catch asleep at the wheel," and log into the BAABCO Sales Development App. It is a category on the App!

- Spend your commissions in advance. . . I dare you . . . The pressure is on!

- Count 10 blessings you have right now. I keep a daily journal to continuously remind me. A lesson from Alicia, my wife.

- Set small, immediate, and achievable growth goals for the day. Delight in your small accomplishments that will bring increase.

- Send a surprise love note to your "someone special." Guys, do this with *no* motive other than to do something nice for her today.

- Remember, your dog's love you unconditionally. Get one if you don't have one. We have two!

- Plan for next week today and not today for today or for tomorrow.

MENTAL WORKOUT QUESTIONS:

1. Who, beside myself, will I strive hard and diligently for today?

_____

_____

_____

_____

2. What negative motivators (fear, procrastination, personal issues) will I put to the side right now so that I can take advantage of this prime time?

_____

_____

_____

_____

SIX-MONTH REVISIT:

How would you answer Questions #1 and #2 above differently today?

1. _____

_____

_____

2. _____

_____

_____

A VISION AND STRATEGY ARE NOT ENOUGH. THE **LONG-TERM KEY TO SUCCESS IS EXECUTION**. EACH DAY. EVERY DAY.

—*Richard M. Kovacevich*

Mental Preparation - Schedule & Execute
Suspects are Preferred

Motivated *"Sales Leader Needed!"* Daily accountability includes: Search out Suspects, identify & profitably justify need for *your* products and services. *Become a Trusted Advisor*. Earn lucrative commissions and enjoy *flexibility!*

Leader, if you are privileged with all of the above in your sales assignment, it is as close as you can get to operating your own business. If you are that fortunate, then you are likely protective over the clients you have worked so diligently to earn. Therefore, elevate your vision to business or franchise owner. You *will* increase your mental attitude when replacing the employee mentality that may be customary. Your new daily approach will grow pride, enthusiasm and income! So, how do you schedule and manage your prospecting? Here are a few of my own best practices:

- Burt's Ten By Ten Daily Net New Prospecting cold calls, completed before 10:00 a.m.

- When possible, choose calls in person rather than teleprospecting. Nothing beats face-to-face contact and the ability to observe your client's place of business, combined with the possibilities of envisioning how your products and services can begin to "live there." This remains true despite today's growing virtual world.

- I have always made it a point to prospect in an area where I am already presenting my products. This is effective in two ways. It cuts your traveling time and expenses. Do NOT get in your car and drive 30 minutes just to procrastinate further if you are already in your assigned area. *Few* exceptions apply to this rule.

- Teleprospecting and video emails can be a great way to cover your area with greater speed than in person. Yet, it is very important to have a good telephone or video voice. Experiment with a colleague like you would during role-playing but, over the phone. Ask for feedback on how you are perceived over the phone or on video.

- Be in the office no later than 7:30 a.m. so that you can address emails, short meetings, research, socializing, etc., and be out of your office and in your franchise or on the phone by 8:30 a.m.

- If your Leader permits, hit the streets before coming in. I assure you, if you meet or exceed your quotas consistently, your leader should not object to your absence in the office and should make you the poster child for all the rest. We live in such a technological world that many emails, meetings, and communications can be handled virtually, via ZOOM, Teams or Webex.

- Keep great records of information and update your data base regularly before 8:30 a.m., after 5:00 p.m., or on weekends only. Do Not allow the administrative requirements of our profession to steal from your prime time.

- Stralectively (strategically and selectively) seek useful public information on your targets. This should be done before 8:30 a.m., after 5:00 p.m., or on the weekends. Remember, committed professionals seldom work M-F and 8-5 only, and they often earn six figure incomes as a result.

NOTES • IDEAS • INSPIRATION

_____

_____

_____

_____

_____

_____

_____

_____

MENTAL WORKOUT QUESTIONS:

1. What does my 30-day Pipeline guarantee about this and next month's results?

_____

_____

_____

_____

2. Have I lived up to my personal best today to be a top & feared Leader among the competing representatives in my franchise?

_____

_____

_____

_____

SIX-MONTH REVISIT:

How would you answer Questions #1 and #2 above differently today?

1. _____

_____

_____

2. _____

_____

_____

THE BATTLEFIELD IS A SCENE
OF CONSTANT CHAOS. THE
WINNER WILL BE THE ONE WHO
CONTROLS THAT CHAOS, BOTH
THEIR OWN AND THE ENEMIES.

—*Napoleon Bonaparte*

Entering the Battlefield
Ready, Aim, Fire!

Strategically planning your work is the first step. However, executing on your plan is the most important component to your success or failure. Experiences have proven to me that being at least 5 days ahead is the most effective way to *successfully* launch a strategy. This way you are in a comfortable atmosphere, you are not easily interrupted by telephone calls, emails, unexpected meetings, or other business interruptions, and you can think clearly and intentionally perform with greater commitment. You will also be able to set your priorities, processes and reflect on them, well in advance.

I have prepared a *sample schedule* for your consideration:

Step 1
Prepared on Thursday for next Thursday:

7:30-8:30 a.m. Clear emails/texts, short and to the point meetings

8:30-10:00 a.m. Burt's Ten By Ten Daily Net New Prospecting

10:00-11:30 a.m. Call or drop in on top suspects and prospects to request presentation, meeting and next action items. Know your top **3** distinctive values. Remember, you are being interviewed by them.

11:30-12:30 p.m. Head to a purposeful lunch/preferably with a top suspect or prospect. Bring a small gift, a book or relevant article.

12:45-1:45 p.m. Closing appointment (Role play mentally on your way to the close). Role plays are dress rehearsals. Prepare with the multiple strategy topics on the BAABCO Sales App.

2:00- 3:00 p.m. Oversee implementation of your latest sale. This does not mean you own the delivery. Allow your delivery personnel to do their job. I recommend you take that time for follow-up calls (in person) to net new suspects in the area of your delivery. Trust me, with your increase of DAILY net new calls you will need as much time as possible for follow-up calls. However, the HUNT comes first.

3:15-5:00 p.m. Continue appointments and follow-up calls to clients, suspects, and prospects.

5:00-6:00 p.m. Activity updates into your CRM from all calls and completed proposals. Send invites with agenda items to upcoming meetings, and catch up to speed on your product knowledge.

Step 2

Check it; does it make sense, does it flow correctly, and is it the best use of your hourly valued time? Your plan may not always be as organized. I will admit I am not always able to list my plan in order of priority or stick to it 100%. But as long as you know what your plan involves, you can work it through, even if your priorities are not listed in sequence. However, once you complete your list, and if it helps you, be sure to number each line item by priority and timeline. I can't stress the importance of having your priorities in order and set before you begin to execute. Accept the fact that agendas do get interrupted. However, by having your agenda in front of you, days ahead, it will motivate you to be more STRALECTIVE as to what interruptions you allow (closings – family) or do not allow (non-urgent proposals).

REALITY POINT

This is all part of time and task management. We all have the same amount of time in a day. What makes you successful and resourceful is how well you make use of your time within proper balance – how effective you are in the short amount of time that you have to be successful. This is also a vital factor in being at the right place at the right time. Because of your professional growth mindset, actions are determined well ahead of time and your results do not depend on luck or winging it.

NOTES • IDEAS • INSPIRATION

_____

_____

_____

_____

_____

_____

_____

_____

MENTAL WORKOUT QUESTIONS:

1. In person, am I seeing two to three suspects/prospects daily in order to guide them to action and closing?

_____

_____

_____

_____

2. Have I evaluated every situation that may be unproductive and is temporarily pulling me away from Daily Net New Prospecting?

_____

_____

_____

_____

SIX-MONTH REVISIT:

How would you answer Questions #1 and #2 above differently today?

1. _____

_____

_____

2. _____

_____

_____

WITHOUT THE USE OF STRATEGIC TONALITIES, COMBINED WITH THE **11- STEP PREDICTABLE SALES PROCESS,** YOU'RE WINGING IT!

—*Paul Martinelli*

Quick and Painless
Shortening Your Selling Cycle

- How are you preparing to Oversee Your Business?
- When did you last assess the value of your hourly time? Is it maintained consistently, or better yet does it increase with constant momentum and year over year?
- Do you know the annual earnings of a top Sales Leader earning 50, 100 or 200 dollars per hour?
- Is this you?

These questions have as many answers as there are reasons for success. In this Profit Pointer let us concentrate on just one particular method of increasing the value of your hourly time.

The Method: Being prepared to do business at all times

The most important factors here are eliminating call-backs and predictably transitioning your prospect-to-client status, while they are immediately closable! As a top Sales Leader you must have the right questions, answers, timing and be equipped, at that moment. This is critical to earning trust and closing the sale now. Capturing the sale sooner will most certainly increase the hourly value of your time.

Now, have you ever experienced the cancellation of what you were certain was a closed sale? The fact that you have a signed agreement does not guarantee that a customer cannot cancel their order if they find (in their perception) something better. In addition, some 30% of verbal commitments do not close at the originally anticipated date, or at all.

Below I have bulleted (for your consideration) some of my best practices to shorten your selling cycle and increase the value of your hourly time.

- Go to the BAABCO App for Shortening the Selling Cycle topic.

- Intentionally know where you are in the Paul Martinelli 11 predictable sales steps, and engagement with your suspect/prospect.

- Set your goal to complete the correct steps, at every engagement, while keeping your suspect/prospect at ease. This is easily said, yet in reality proves to be delicate surgery. **Trust in You is key.**

- Confirm with your contact (if they are an influencer) that they have the full support of their C-Level Leaders to pursue and take timely action, with the right solution.

- Reconfirm timelines for closure contingent upon your committed & agreed offerings - solutions. The offerings can be confirmed by utilizing your BURTISMS aka open and close ended questions. Go to the BAABCO app now to study the BURTISMS.

- Determine and gain early acceptance for the factors that are in play and lead up to a favorable decision. These include Product, Brand, Financing, Limited Offers, Timing, Ultimate Signer, Desire, Service, Urgency, Ease of Implementation and YOU!

A TOP SALES LEADER IS **EQUIPPED** WITH THE RIGHT QUESTIONS, ANSWERS, AND TIMING TO CLOSE AT THE RIGHT MOMENT.

- Never state more than three benefits without utilizing your BURTISMS. And never overlook an "aha" moment without the use of your BURTISMS.

- Ask for and confirm support of your offer at every in-person, phone, or virtual engagement.

- Establish at the 1st meeting if the decision is based on price only, a hurry up and get it done mentality or overall best value. If you do none of the other nine, please be sure to complete this one. Otherwise, you may lose critical rapport and not regain it.

- Ask for and receive affirmations for closure from the very first meeting or cold call. Be prepared to close on the go if they say "yes" on the spot. YES!

REALITY POINT

All Professional Sales Leaders should follow the Paul Martinelli 11 Steps of the Predictable Sales Process in order to achieve profitable closure. However, in many cases, the Top Sales Leaders complete the same steps TWICE as FAST. This is because they are masters at establishing rapport and building a trusted advisor – client relationship. This is evidence of what I call "Catching the Competition Asleep at the Wheel." This strategy topic is presented on the BAABCO Sales App.

MENTAL WORKOUT QUESTIONS:

1. Do I know the importance between how the meeting ended and not merely how it went?

_____

_____

_____

_____

2. What will I do differently today to start increasing my hourly earnings and the value of my time?

_____

_____

_____

_____

SIX-MONTH REVISIT:

How would you answer Questions #1 and #2 above differently today?

1. _____

_____

_____

2. _____

_____

_____

YOU CAN HAVE ANYTHING
YOU WANT IN LIFE IF YOU
DRESS FOR IT.

—*Edith Head*

Committed to Owning It
Look the Part

Leader, would you buy a new sports car from someone dressed like the Good Humor Man? Would you trust an interior decorator dressed like an employee at the local post office? The answer to these questions is probably "no." Whatever your business, you should know what it takes to look and be the part. There are three critical factors here. Your attire, hygiene and business acumen. By this I mean your hair, teeth, breath, nails, posture, gestures, soft skills, tonalities, communication style and grammar. These are personal details you must have a vested interest in and can generally control.

If you agree this is important, I encourage you to seek some constructive feedback regarding your "look" from trusted friends, loved ones or colleagues. Do this before your sales leader volunteers their opinion.

As a former leader of sales teams, I considered it as important to constructively coach our sales people as it was to catch them doing things right. This meant complimenting them when they looked like a million dollars or advising them when they looked like a million, after taxes! The most important reason to do this is for your success. If you are in a business where proper dress and executive presence matter, then do your best to always look and be the part.

To quote a mentor of mine and highly talented sales leader:

> " Dress as if your attire is part of your compensation plan. "

—Anonymous

When you look the part, you are likely to own the right attitude. They go hand in hand. This is in large part why the prospect will seek you to lead them and invest, in you. Your attitude aligns to self-confidence, professionalism, integrity, trust and the right expertise. In Profit Pointer # 1 when I referred to the competition? It is there, and you are not the only one with a great product, brand, or service.

Therefore, you must also sell yourself, and this is done in part through a positive and visual attitude. It is important to point out that I do not mean with a pretentious demeanor. You must

GET COMFORTABLE AND IN THE HABIT OF **ROLE-PLAYING** WITH COLLEAGUES. WE CALL IT THE ESSENTIAL DRESS REHEARSAL.

become adaptable and know when to be the assertive leader, the excellent listener, the enthusiastic trusted advisor and the ultimate deliverer of measurable results. In many cases, you must be all of them with one prospect. This knowledge can often be portrayed through attitude. Attitude is critical; it is what makes you believable or unbelievable. When it comes to gaining the confidence of your prospect, unbelievable is not the place to be.

Additionally, do get in the habit of ROLE-PLAYING in front of a mirror and/or with colleagues. This will help you determine if you do look the part and portray the right attitude. It is an investment in your most valued asset . . . You. Remember, Role Plays are the Dress Rehearsals that will increase the probability of your sales.

REALITY POINT

I have been fortunate to count on our daughter to give me her thumbs up or down once I'm suited up for the day. Her advice is essential to helping me look the part in my business career.

MENTAL WORKOUT QUESTIONS:

1. Did I look at myself in the mirror (top to bottom) after I dressed for today?

_____

_____

_____

_____

2. Was I impressed?

_____

_____

_____

_____

SIX-MONTH REVISIT:

How would you answer Questions #1 and #2 above differently today?

1. _____

_____

_____

2. _____

_____

_____

THERE ARE RISKS AND COSTS TO ACTION. BUT THEY ARE **FAR LESS THAN THE LONG-RANGE RISKS** OF COMFORTABLE INACTION.

—*John F. Kennedy*

Intentional — Purposeful Action
Getting Out of Your Office

*Are you a **Story Teller** or a **Story Maker**?*

A great way to determine this is to observe your associates. Study how effectively they make use of their time while at the office, on the road, in front of a prospect or working from home.

Are they productive or are they procrastinating and avoiding the most challenging yet, most lucrative part of their sales profession?

Leaving the office to prospect for new business may lead to getting the painful slap in the face by a cold sales preventer, as I refer to them. You have to respond by thinking clearly and getting back on your feet quickly in order to get them on your side and have them guide you to the right C-level Executive (CEO, CFO, CIO, CMO, COO, etc.). Look at your associates objectively and then compare their actions and results to yours. Now decide: How will You make that transition from Story Teller to Story Maker?

Leader, this is, where The Art of Professional Prospecting is rooted. This is a self-coachable moment for you. You see, despite how much you know, how well you communicate, how well you dress, or how capable your skills, nothing matters unless you get out of your office and Shout-It-Out!

I have coached Sales Leaders to "do it your own way", or have mentored others to "be creative", provided they can show me a fat, healthy, consistent 30-day pipeline. Show me new names and do not discuss the same no action prospects week after week. Wouldn't you agree, the toughest competitor in your industry probably gets more "no, thank yous" than anyone else does? Sure, they do. And that is because of their market penetration. They have more reps out of the office and in their territories than anyone. Because of this, they also get more "yes, thank yous" than you may. If your company a tough market competitor then you know precisely my meaning and intention.
 I have kept the point of this Profit Pointer simple. Now, I will further coach, mentor and motivate you to get out of the office. Here are some proven and best disciplines that you will relate to.

When planning your work, itemize the moment in which you plan to leave the office. Leader, this Profit Pointer has an additional message from Profit Pointer #5. A line item was intentionally left out on that agenda. It is the most important one . . . and that is inserting a specific timeline directing you to leave the office or computer screen! You must visually embrace and execute it on your agenda (planned 5 working days ahead). It will give you a huge confirmation of accomplishment to execute action, that which is your responsibility to yourself, team and your employer. Remember, you are a Hired Gun. Get out there and complete your assignment! This action is discussed further in The Ten By Ten Daily Net New Prospecting Strategy form.

Too often we allow ourselves to get distracted by emails, social media, calls, texts, proposals, strategy meetings, webinars, or socializing when we should be doing Daily Net New Prospecting. This strategy, however basic in its exercise, will help to make your next direction and action, the obvious one.

A few Should-Dos for your success:

1. Meet with a colleague in your territory at a set time so as to obligate you to leave the office.
2. Get yourself a cheerleader (spouse, coach, mentor, leader) who knows your game plan and will help keep you accountable toward your new accomplishments. It is the basic purpose of leaving the office. This BURTISM is line-itemed at BAABCO.biz/ten-by-ten
3. Keep an open agenda with your sales leader. They did not hire you to fail. Your success is their success. Work this strategy together for best results.

REALITY POINT

Obligate yourself (on your daily calendar/outlook) to leave the office at a set time, usually at 8:30 a.m. This should be an action step. Every recommendation above delivers a confirmed accountability and accomplishment with regard to yourself, your sales leader, a loved one, or a colleague. The end result is that disciplined commitment to this task will propel you to reach the essential growth goal of closing more business, consistently and profitably.

Remember this, Sales Professional. Sales reps rarely get terminated for incompetence. They are more often terminated for lack of production. This is often due to their lack and full ownership of Net New Prospecting, resulting from their activities in the previous 60 to 90 days.

You can view my illustrations at **BAABCO.biz/graph.**

MENTAL WORKOUT QUESTIONS:

1. Did I plan for today within the last 24 hours?

_____

_____

_____

_____

2. Had I planned for today five days ago, how much more committed and productive would I be today?

_____

_____

_____

_____

SIX-MONTH REVISIT:

How would you answer Questions #1 and #2 above differently today?

1. _____

_____

_____

2. _____

_____

_____

YOU ARE A HIRED GUN...
YOU COME TO TOWN,
ELIMINATE THE COMPETITION,
AND TAKE OVER.

—*Burt Villarreal*

Taking Over!
Growing Your Territory (Franchise)

What we are aiming for is a transformation and total awareness, through Daily Net New Prospecting. Thus, understanding how we can become more impactful through gained knowledge and experience.

Early on, I mentioned becoming more effective through our experiences. We can cite examples such as having worked equally as hard the previous year, and yet succeeding at making considerably more income, this year. We concluded you are, smarter and listen actively, quicker to overcome, deflect or avoid objections, and more effective, through learned experiences. However, this is ultimately the result of good habits and learning from the cumulative wins and losses. We have emphasized the best habit being, a proper balance of Daily Net New Prospecting, which entails working the territory, and it must be done intelligently. To achieve this level, it must be put into practice in such a way which reflects total awareness in your efforts. Then and only then will it emerge to, the Art of Professional Prospecting.

Documentation and tracking software products (BAABCO Sales App, Sales Force, Sales Chain or Monday.com) play very important factors here. Through documentation and tracking you will become more knowledgeable of the prospect's present and future needs, and prepared when the time is right. Ask as many open questions as time will allow during your cold calling and telemarketing. Commitment to product knowledge by vertical and trustful storytelling are paramount.

The best questions to ask lead to your products and stimulate interest in their minds. Ask open creative questions. In the end, organization will help to keep you abreast of all this information and make it readily available. Keep all of your data organized either by next contact date, vertical markets, C-Level contacts, influencers, annual revenues, usage, current technology, introduction date, service contract expirations or pain points – just to name a few categories.

Upon making the full rounds of your current territory (except move ins-move outs) you will never again need to ask yourself: "Where do I prospect today?" The path of certainty will have been laid out for you through your own strategic planning. You will own all of your follow up contact dates at your fingertips and within vertical markets if you wish. The idea behind this handbook is to show you simplicity. No complicated formulas here... Just no wiggle room.

REALITY POINT

Be sure to have new and exciting news when contacting suspects and prospects. This would be, a fresh concept to enhance their business with your new product or service. Perhaps, you could mention someone in their field who just joined your organization (as a new client) and how they are now benefiting from your consulting, products, and servicing. The more beneficial and exciting your news, the greater your chances of them eagerly connecting with you when the receptionist tells them that you are holding on line 1. In other words, Sales Professional, you are continuously leading and earning the right to be a high contender for their business!

NOTES • IDEAS • INSPIRATION

_____
_____
_____
_____
_____
_____
_____
_____

MENTAL WORKOUT QUESTIONS:

1. How often do my suspects, prospects and clients see or hear from me on an annual basis?

_____

_____

_____

_____

2. Am I superior to the competing Sales Leaders in my franchise in earning the right to be a high contender for my suspect's or prospect's future business?

_____

_____

_____

_____

SIX-MONTH REVISIT:

How would you answer Questions #1 and #2 above differently today?

1. _____

_____

_____

2. _____

_____

_____

IT'S THE LAW OF AVERAGES:
**PUT IN MORE, COME OUT
WITH MORE**.

—*Bruce Lee*

Know Your Own Metrics
Truth in Numbers

Your industry has a conversion formula for determining (on average) how many prospecting calls are required to set one qualified appointment. This is followed by a formula for the average number of appointments, assessments or proposals required to make the sale. These are generally very basic and time proven metrics.

It is very important that you know not only the average metrics, but that you monitor your own. The average Sales Leader will probably fall much within those industry metrics. Many of the top Sales Leaders will likely maintain different ratios (or not). I say this because many of them consider themselves average closers. Their continued success is fueled by their healthy 30-day Pipeline. If you are not familiar with these average metrics, then obtain them from your Sales Leader. Be sure to compare your numbers with the average metrics. The results should be of high interest to you and clearly tell you whether you are working a job or establishing a strong basis for a successful sales career, fueled with tremendous accomplishments.

PROFIT POINTER

REALITY POINT

If you accurately monitor YOUR metrics, you can closely determine your future income.

NOTES • IDEAS • INSPIRATION

MENTAL WORKOUT QUESTIONS:

1. How many sales (transactions) have I made and lost in the last 3 months?

_____

_____

_____

_____

2. Do I have certainty now, that I must rebalance my Daily Net New Prospecting in order to grow the number of weekly first-time appointments and monthly transactions I close going forward?

_____

_____

_____

_____

SIX-MONTH REVISIT:

How would you answer Questions #1 and #2 above differently today?

1. _____

_____

_____

2. _____

_____

_____

I LEARNED TO GO INTO BUSINESS ONLY WITH **PEOPLE WHOM I LIKE,** TRUST AND ADMIRE.

—*Warren Buffett*

Establishing Instant Rapport
Building Trusted Advisor Relationships

What is the difference between a business professional and an amateur? Professionals plan for their successes and are compensated to the best of their willingness and abilities. Professionals are committed to acquiring additional education to continuously pilot toward high achievement. An amateur has not yet achieved or may never have the intense desire required to achieve the excellent status in a business, where the highest compensation is earned by those who are fully committed and engaged for the long term.

Are you a Professional or an Amateur?

Suppose your competitors referenced your name and included a few descriptive words. For example, would trusted advisor, integrity, transparent, expert, tenured, successful, accountable, effective, influencer, mentor, consultative, competitive, respectful, courteous, or excellent communicator be mentioned? These words are vital for enabling you to be viewed as a Professional Sales Leader.

So why are so many professionals still not closing more sales? Because they fail to establish instant Rapport:

Why is instant Rapport a Vital Organ to Your Success?

Because establishing instant Rapport is the first step necessary in leading you to complete the 11 steps of the predictable sales model. Paul Martinelli states that Sales, at its highest level, is the transference of emotion. This emotion is certainty. Rapport is accomplished through certainty in you as the product expert, problem solver, and confident communicator who operates with trust and integrity.

Paul defines Rapport as a healthy relationship between two parties who understand each other's feelings or ideas. These understandings serve them well in communicating effectively and successfully. An essential success formula for a prospect and seller!

Reflect on that statement for a moment. Is it not true that when you won your recent transaction, your client rapport evolved into a trusting relationship that included a very high level of certainty with you? Perhaps, there were good conversations of commonality between the client and you that were unrelated to business.

However, in the end, you made the sale because you established yourself as the expert and trusted advisor. You delivered certainty in solving their pain points by actively listening, and each commitment you made during the sales process was fulfilled exactly how you said it would be. This is Rapport in action!

I bring continued awareness to the word Rapport because one is at high risk in attempting first to build commonality if the prospect does not feel it is sincere and only a ploy to get one's business. Therefore, I urge you to establish Rapport before attempting to find commonalities. Rapport is established in part by opening with non-evasive to more relevant questions, about their business and goals.

PROFESSIONALS PLAN FOR THEIR **SUCCESSES** AND ARE COMPENSATED TO THE BEST OF THEIR WILLINGNESS, INTEGRITY, AND ABILITIES.

Examples: Rapport building - open & close-ended questions:

- Can I ask you a few questions to better serve you?
- Do I have your right cell #...email address...spelling?
- What factors contributed to your recent company growth?
- What challenging trends are impacting your industry?
- Why did you take the time to meet with me today?
- What is your vision for the company in two to five years?
- What is needed to take the company to the next level?

REALITY POINT

Paul Martinelli states; Sales people may often lose the ultimate opportunity because they confuse Rapport with Commonality. Leader, know and apply the difference. In addition, stay genuinely excited about your product, services, company, and the Why of your value proposition. Remember, Excitement is contagious.

These are just a few questions you can ask to help your prospect move to feel comfortable and proud to expand. These questions will get them excited, emotionally engaged, and eager to share more about their business and themselves.

Once you have listened, acknowledge them and begin to form those business commonalities (verbally). For example, if they answer: "We have been in business ten years, are locally owned, and deliver better service than our competition by not using voice mails or charging hidden fees." Well, you should start talking about how your company mirrors most if not all of those attributes. Remember, speak and be genuine in your responses. People will trust their feelings when they witness evidence of your genuineness. Once you have established and continue building Rapport, I recommend incorporating light commonalities, if applicable.

Suppose you are in a sales cycle that typically lasts two to four months or longer. In that case, I recommend that you do not attempt to establish the personal commonalities until the second or third in-person or virtual meeting. Remember Sales Leader, keep it light until you have established consistent Rapport, Trust and Certainty in you, during the selling process.

Below are examples of questions or statements for building light commonalities:

- Did you catch that game over the weekend?
- That's a great color (dress, suit) on you.
- Have you tried that new restaurant?
- Do you golf-fish-hike-workout-read books?
- Are your children attending grammar or high school?

I expect you to now grasp why success in business relationships is best achieved by first building Rapport professionally and genuinely. By accomplishing such a foundation, you may also find that your business may become more about desired and respectable profit margins and not only about price. People value genuine relationships with merchants and their employees. Many Professional Sales Leaders of all sectors enjoy an abundance of business and healthy margins partly because of their genuine Rapport and earned relationships.

NOTES • IDEAS • INSPIRATION

MENTAL WORKOUT QUESTIONS:

1. Yes or No. Have I established, built, and maintained Rapport with my 30-day closable prospects?

_____

_____

_____

_____

2. Yes or No. Do my 30-day closable prospects see me as their Expert, Trusted Advisor who can solve their pain point?

_____

_____

_____

_____

SIX-MONTH REVISIT:

How would you answer Questions #1 and #2 above differently today?

1. _____

_____

_____

2. _____

_____

_____

IN THE END, WE ONLY REGRET THE CHANCES WE DID NOT TAKE.

—*Lewis Carroll*

Reality Sets In
The Painful Slap in the Face

Also Known As:

- "No Soliciting."
- "No thank you."
- "Call Security."
- "We are too busy."
- "You are the tenth sales rep today."
- "We are not interested."

Leader, I personally understand the following:

- "It's not in the budget."
- "Decisions are not made locally."
- "Maybe next year."
- "We work by appointment only."

I understand because the latter, softer rejections are challenges that are easier to endure and emerge from. They provide an opportunity to engage in a brief discussion in order to begin building rapport and collaboration. However, the first objections are programmed to be immediately curt, and to make you feel intimidated or disinterested. They are very unwelcoming to us; even for Sales Warriors who work very hard and execute on strategies to truly help prospects realize the many benefits of doing business with us. However, with a Healthy 30-Day Pipeline we can easily exclude or patiently work within the first six.

Bonus: Overcoming the Well-known, yet Unspoken, Admitted Truth of FEAR

FEAR is a problem which I firmly believe, a very high majority of prospecting Sales Leaders are unfortunately afflicted with. Let me elaborate. Perhaps you label it as procrastination, as being too busy following up with current opportunities in your pipeline, checking emails, delivering proposals, handling problematic clients, or paralysis from analysis. The list goes on. However, I believe from personal experience that it comes down to FEAR. A psychological FEAR of what you now realize I call the painful slap in the face, or the FEAR of the rejection examples I stated at the onset of this Profit Pointer. So how do you overcome FEAR? Or more importantly, how do you overcome FEAR today, as well for the rest of your days as a Professional Sales Leader?

Competitive Tactics - How to Conquer and Destroy FEAR

1. Commit to a date and time for taking action to get out of your current comfort zone. How about today?

2. Initiate and complete Self Talks on your voice mail and listen to them at least once per day.

3. Initiate and complete Self-Faith Talks on your voice mail and listen to them at least once per day, assuming you pray.

4. Envision your retirement; put today's FEAR aside if it does not meet your expectations.

5. Picture working through the age of 85, because you will have to unless you defeat FEAR.

6. Jump or be pushed into the deep end. Recall Profit Pointer #8 and why most sales representatives are fired. It is not for incompetency.

7. Do not proactively call existing clients for one week. Take the time for, Daily Net New Prospecting. I double dare you!

8. Dare to walk into your boss' boss' office and ask them, "How am I doing?" If scheduled, they are known as skip level meetings.

9. Go to the restroom and start sparring with yourself in the mirror. It will give you stamina and desire!

10. Remember who depends on you financially. Now, through the Law of Intention, go and make them even prouder today.

REALITY POINT

"First of all, let me assert my firm belief that the only thing we have to fear is fear itself – nameless, unreasoning, unjustified terror which paralyzes needed efforts to convert retreat into advance." Franklin D. Roosevelt, March 4th, 1933.

MENTAL WORKOUT QUESTIONS:

1. Have I been truthful to myself as to why I hesitate to Net New Prospect (HUNT) on a daily basis?

_____

_____

_____

_____

2. What will I do differently, starting right now, to conquer this newly identified hesitation?

_____

_____

_____

_____

SIX-MONTH REVISIT:

How would you answer Questions #1 and #2 above differently today?

1. _____

_____

_____

2. _____

_____

_____

I WILL **NEVER APOLOGIZE** FOR BEING A HUNTER.

—*Eva Shockey*

Search, Find, and Destroy the Competition

Burt's Ten By Ten Daily Net New Prospecting Strategy

My ultimate communication to you in this guidebook, is for you to visualize the critical need to first properly balance your Daily Net New Prospecting over follow-up calls vs. prospecting or selling techniques. After all, only minimal information has been dedicated to techniques with potential clients. I have seen too many talented and personable sales people who lack success despite great prospecting techniques. For now, please be certain of the evidential basis of my message.

I speak with many Business Owners, Vice Presidents of Sales, Directors of Sales, Sales Managers, and Sales Leaders who (once we dissect the actual activity level of Net New Prospecting) agree: The majority of inconsistent or low sales production is due to insufficient Net New Prospecting! As well, too many reps cling to their Hopefuls way too long.

In other words, many reps have a tendency to stay overly busy on the four to seven necessary follow-up calls (just to identify a suspect or prospect) and ignore or overlook the critical need for Daily Net New Prospecting aka the HUNT. I label it as unbalanced Net New Prospecting.

As a result, their 30-60-90 Day Pipeline is usually at 50-70% of where it needs to be and will not achieve sustainable sales success. In addition, many of them suffer (as do their sales managers) from the up and down roller coaster of month-to-month productivity. Please refer to BAABCO.biz/graph for further confirmation.

Upon review, you will see the illustration of unbalanced activity to unproductive results. If this illustration looks personally familiar, it is likely due to your lack of Daily Net New Prospecting. You are off balance! You must take action on the Hunt vs. the Farming.

So, Leader, I ask you:

- Does this seem all too familiar?
- How does below quota performance impact your ability to sell at solid or higher profit margins?
- How frustrating are today's results to you and your family?
- How can you plan for a prosperous future vs. mediocre results?

I know that I have insisted enough on the pain points. However, you must reflect deeply because the consequences of an unbalanced and insufficient Daily Net New Prospecting strategy...are real.

So, how do we grow from here?

- How do you empower and commit yourself to double or triple your Net New Prospecting?
- How do you identify and take ownership of a net new call vs. a follow-up call? Do you know the difference?
- What habits will you rebalance to control this behavioral change?
- What will this mean to your Income?
- How will it expand your new focus on Value vs. Price Buyer's
- When do you realize the new results on your commissions checks?

First Things First:

BELOW ARE 8 COMPETITIVE TACTICS TO GET YOU STARTED. Be advised, there is no wiggle room.

1 **You commit to Burt's Ten By Ten Daily Net New Prospecting Strategy.** If other strategies are getting you two thousand five hundred Net New Prospecting Calls annually in your territory and working great for you monthly and year over year, then give this guide book to a friend who will benefit from it.

2 **Honestly identify routines you currently do from 8:30-10:00.** It is highly likely these routines consist of follow-up calls, texts, social media, proposals, emails, training, Teams meetings, Zoom calls, travel time, non- closing appointments, or socializing. Eliminate those activities from 8:30-10:00 a.m. This adjustment period may take you – at most – two weeks, since I do not recommend canceling appointments you already have set before starting your new Ten By Ten Daily Net New Prospecting Strategy.

3 **Clearly understand my definition of a Net New Call.** A Net New Call is a non-customer, previous customer, or existing customer you have not called on in 90 days. The ongoing (necessary) three to seven follow-up calls to someone you previously cold called in the last day, week, month, or 90 days (suspect, prospect, or customer) are excluded from this newly rebalanced formula.

4 **You embrace what I call the Prize of the New-Found Five.** That is, start your day no later than 7:30 a.m. and or stay until 5:30 p.m. Utilize this time to address emails, proposals, CRM, meetings, socializing and such. In addition, commit to, two-and-one half hours over the weekend for strategy planning, product knowledge, proposals, or continuous education. Leader, these five extra hours will be needed to make room for the Net New Prospecting you are now completing between 8:30 and 10:00 a.m. LET'S DO THIS!

5 **Get ready to earn your way to a higher tax bracket.** Seriously, during the sales coaching's of the Ten By Ten Daily Net New Prospecting, I often ask groups what would happen to their income if they doubled their rolling 30 day Pipeline in the near future. Too often someone falls into my trap and says, "It would double my income." I say: Wrong!

6 **Believe that your income could nearly triple.** Here's why: IF tomorrow you were blessed (by your good efforts) with twice as many 30-day closable prospects as you may have today, I believe you would become more stralective (strategic and selective) in who You committed your time to. You would gravitate toward your prospects (suspects preferred) who are making a buying decision based on overall best value and not just price. And as a result, your sales transactions would likely double and the profit margins on those sales would increase significantly because of where you have now decided to focus your attention: the now evident abundance of Value Buyers. Please log into the category of Value Over Price for further validation on the BAABCO Sales App.

7 **You commit 60 to 120 days (initially) to the Ten By Ten Daily Net New Prospecting Strategy.** You will however see results almost immediately (likely within two weeks.) The immediate results will be seen in an increase of future opportunities. You will start filling up with first time appointments and new names that were not already in your Pipeline. As you come upon the 30 to 60 and 90-day mark you will see your Pipeline filling up with real closing opportunities within the next 30 to 60 day cycle. You should find yourself firing Prospects from your follow-up call list because you are now too busy with real buyers as a direct result of your Ten By Ten Daily Net New Prospecting Strategy.

8 **Do not over shoot.** The Strategy is Ten By Ten Daily Net New Calls, not 30 by noon or 40 by end of day. If you complete your quality Ten Net New Calls in person before 10:00 a.m., then start on your other responsibilities for the day. Understand this, Sales Leader. The Ten By Ten Strategy is a professional and personal choice and life commitment. It becomes an intricate part of your ownership to, consistently increasing daily, monthly, and annual successes. Self - Accountability is key. You will now need the rest of the day for your required follow- up calls and added transaction closings.

Now, let me introduce you to the coveted Ten By Ten Daily Net New Prospecting form & process. Pause for a moment, download the form from the BAABCO Sales App. Leader, I am a firm believer in the basic fundamentals of selling and if it's not broken don't fix it. I emphasize this because the form you are about to be introduced to has served me well for many years. I often say in my coaching sessions that while products and services have changed dramatically in the last two, five, ten, and twenty years, many of the proven fundamentals for successful professional sales have not. That being said, you will find the form quite basic. In Profit Pointer #9, I clearly stated: "There are no complicated formulas here." The same holds true to the Ten By Ten Form. However, make no mistake. While simple in its appearance, it has been prepared to challenge you, both professionally and personally. Under few exceptions certain parts of the form may be substituted with your CRM. The BAABCO App tracker features monitoring as well.

The following is a detailed step-by-step explanation of each component of the Ten By Ten Daily Net New Prospecting Form. I recommend you follow the form as I strategically break it down for you. We start at the very top of the form with Ten By Ten. Ten Net New Calls Daily by 10:00 a.m. Do the math. Based on 50 weeks in a year (deducting your two weeks of vacation), you will accumulate 2,500 net new calls annually. If that is what you accomplished in the last 12 months, then I congratulate you; now go ahead and give this guide book to a friend who needs it.

I continue to emphasize "Net New." This was defined for you earlier in this Profit Pointer. The commitment (or lack there-of) to Net New activity is where we separate the Professionals from the Amateurs. Remember, compensation was distinctly separated between the two. In addition, we identified that many average closers are consistently above plan because of their healthy Pipeline, which goes hand in hand with healthy prospecting habits. Sadly, many great closers are consistently way below plan because they lack in Net New Activity. Now, let's study the words of wisdom to bring you into the right growth mindset...where Failure is Not an Option.

Are You Being Out Sold or Out Prospected?

Unfortunately, many sales reps blame everyone but themselves. However, if they had tripled their net new activity 60 to 90 days ago, they would realize the very different and positive results it has on this month's production. A great lesson from Dad. Log into the BAABCO Sales App & the Ten by Ten form with graph link NOW.

Consistent, Quality, New Activity Produces Consistent Productivity

I illustrated the consequences of one on the other earlier in this Profit Pointer. In fact, it is generally mirrored. Today's production results, high or low, generally mirror prospecting activity 60 to 90 days ago in a selling cycle that lasts two to four months. Some of the great closers I have described falter by ignoring net new activity while they are experiencing high production months. That is where the roller coaster of month-to-month production, is most evident. Suddenly, two catastrophic months unfold which were preceded by two great months, and it all happened because no one was minding the tasks of Daily Net New Activity. Sound familiar? See the illustration graph on the BAABCO Sales App now.

A Ship is Safe in Harbor. But That is Not a Ship's Purpose

Remember the Hired Gun mindset in the BAABCO Sales App? Please see sales questions #82 and video on the BAABCO App for further information. Keep in mind the Fear Theory and why many sales representatives do not prospect? We tend to feel safe at our desks or in front of existing customers or situations. Anyone can be paid a basic salary for those activities. However, the big commissions come when we emerge out of our comfort zones. And remember, a ship that stays in harbor too long begins to rust. Do not let yourself get rusty at Prospecting for Suspects. Make sense?

It is Easier to Steer a Moving Vehicle vs. a Non-Moving Vehicle

I'm certain you have noticed the difference. And once you start moving it sure does get easier to move that steering wheel, right? As a matter of fact, it gets to be fun and it beats walking. Yes, I said fun. There is no better feeling than completing this utmost duty to yourself during the first part of your day . . . Net New Prospecting for your professional and personal success. Truly, you will find that hitting your territory early and daily is a great way to earn and laugh your way to the bank! Another great lesson from Dad.

Date:
This is critical to your success. It is about "Daily", not every other day or a couple of times per week. As a result, your form should indicate "Daily" entries. If you are not seeing Daily entries after one week, you are not following the Strategy or Spirit and you will not experience consistent results. A tracker is available to you on the BAABCO Sales App. Now Recommit & start over immediately.

Start Time:

Another crucial component is starting on time. If after a week your entries show starts of 10:30, 1:00, or 4:00 . . . you have misplaced the very spirit of the Ten By Ten Strategy. Start time is 8:30 a.m. This is every day unless you are on a closing appointment, a demo where you will attempt to close, in bed sick, at a funeral (yours or someone else's), a loved one is sick, on vacation, having a baby, or your significant other is having the baby. You get the message: all previous routines from 8:30 to 10:00 as stated earlier, stop when you commit to and apply, The Ten By Ten Daily Net New Prospecting Strategy.

YOUR NEW PACE WILL HAVE YOU **RUNNING AT TOP SPEED,** SO TAKE THAT EXTRA TIME TO COMPLETE YOUR FOLLOW-UP DUTIES.

End Time:

Shoot for ten quality cold calls. There will be days during which you complete the cold calls in 20 or 30 minutes. Mostly you are looking to complete them by 10:00 a.m. This will help to ensure quality calls. If you finish early, do not overshoot. Your new pace will have you running at top speed so take that extra time to complete your follow-up duties. It's Ten By Ten daily. That's it. The greater you know your products and by vertical market, the longer it will take you to complete your 10 in person calls. And that's what you want...Quality calls. Am I Right?

To:

My favorite: Who will you share your new plan with for greater and long-term success? Will it be your spouse, your sweetheart, your child, a mentor, your boss, a friend, a colleague, or the person in the mirror? Either way, I recommend you share this new goal with someone who can be your cheerleader as you grow forward. This will work, even if you are your own cheer leader!

The next section identifies your Daily Ten Net New calls. These entries should be put into your database before 8:30, after 5:00 or on the weekends. Please utilize the choices of Suspect, Prospect, Recall, Cold or Appointment to help you identify your future calls from today's calls. COLD signifies no immediate opportunity. That is unless you have additional products, solutions, or services to propose. The Appointment line is there because you should expect to land more Appointments on the go as a result of having doubled or tripled your Net New Prospecting activity. Getting excited? You should be! We are about to start making some serious money . . . and consistently! Most of these activities can be digitally tracked on your BAABCO Sales App or CRM platform.

Daily Comments:

You are sharp as a tack, the strategist, tactician, commander, rocket scientist, Golden Sales Leader of your (territory) franchise. I've often commented during coaching: "If you owned 10 Jimmy John's sandwich shops and overheard a commercial from your neighbor who owns 10 Jason's Deli sandwich shops, would you stop and listen? I certainly hope so. You must know as often as possible what your competition is up to. During your cold calling or telemarketing, take the time to improve the quality of the call by asking a few questions. Find out who is having issues or being praised for the customer service provided? Which of your competitors are having challenges delivering products, parts, solutions, inventory, or providing timely service? What competitors are discounting heavy on transactions? What competitor is offering the best perceived value and earning a premium?

Leader, the Ten By Ten form is utilized to guide you to staying on track daily. That is the only way to measure your consistency or inconsistency. The form is timely even in actuality. This is because I have yet to see an automated way of reminding you of what you did not do yesterday. Even your CRM database software may not say: "Hey, where have you been these last few days?" or "You have not made one Net New entry in a whole week." Therefore, the PDF form that reminds you "Daily" of your success or failure to make Ten Net New Calls by 10:00 a.m. is a valuable tool. You also have the digital version in the BAABCO App tracker.

To summarize Sales Leader, this is your new beginning. I hope you will fully embrace it as such. Your success with this strategy is also my success. Changing habits and, most importantly, applying them on to your life immediately, is not always easy. However, you know what's next. You know what I am about to say: Anything that legitimately brings you increased and sustainable success is worth the extra effort invested to accomplish that success! Agreed? Agreed!

Change can be challenging. If you have any doubts, I urge you to go to Profit Pointer # 3 on Motivation and review the 20 competitive tactics, as well the mental workout questions I detailed to GET YOU MOTIVATED. Review them daily if needed. I recommend that you embrace your favorite 5 as YOUR starting point.

Have a Profitable Day Professional Sales Leader and please continue on to Profit Pointer #14 where I share more of my personal Best Practices for long-term and growing success.

TRUE SUCCESS IS OVERCOMING THE FEAR OF BEING UNSUCCESSFUL.

—Paul Sweeney

A Sales Leader's Journal
Success By Strategic Intentionality

Leader, we come to the conclusion of *The Art of Professional Prospecting*. I trust that it has delivered fresh ideas, challenged you and served you well as a reminder to the required fundamentals that build an emerging and enduring success in a professional sales career.

In short, assuming you possess certain skill sets, it does not only matter how skillful you are in front of a suspect or prospect. What matters most is how many, Net New Quality Calls you execute to consistently build and maintain your Pipeline. This will help you to avoid the frustration of the monthly 30-day roller coaster we see too often in the business of professional sales. I was very clear in illustrating the multiple anxieties that occur in Profit Pointer #13. Take the time to review them again if needed. They are designed to serve as hard and strategic reminders when applicable.

Below are my final highlights and recommended best practices for your benefit. I look forward to hearing from you and learning of your increased successes on the Battlefield. Please stay in touch, enthusiastic and ambitious! Feel free to contact me directly through the BAABCO Sales Training and Development App!

1 **Ten By Ten Daily Net New Prospecting**. It is a way of life. Ten By Ten Daily equals 50 per week and 2,500 annually. These are not to be combined with follow-up calls. A Net New is someone you have not connected with in 90 days. This includes past, present or future clients. If your plan has not enabled you to consistently grow, meet or exceed quota for three years running then commit to Burt's Ten By Ten.

2 **The Prize of the New Found Five.** At your desk by 7:30 or stay until 5:30. In addition, invest no less than two and a half hours over the weekend. You just gained 5 hours outside of your 8:30 to 10:00 calendar for Net New Prospecting time to then focus on emails, CRM, proposals, meetings or continued professional development.

3 **Log into the BAABCO Sales App!** Where else can you instantly review over 150 strategic sales questions and to - the - point answers for what you need most to anticipate before, during, and after the sales process? Take a moment today to log in and enjoy the profitable benefits.

4 **Treat every day as if it is the last day of the month.** Most of your competitors will not, yet at least one will. Get comfortable with "no", as clients are not likely to say "yes" right away. Remember, ask for the order early and perhaps more than once or twice. This is a part of the Predictable Sales Process Model.

5 **Shorten the Selling Cycle.** Know the steps of the selling process well, where you are in those steps, and learn to move with trust and confidence. The Ten By Ten will keep you so busy that shortening the selling cycle must become strategic. Assume you have at least one competitor on the same mission and intentionally "catch the competition asleep at the wheel." These strategies are high-priority in the BAABCO Sales App.

6 **Live by the 20/30 Rule.** That is, 20 Closable Prospects every 30 days. The statistics show evidence that on average, five will move to next month, five will do nothing at all, five you will lose and five you will win. Cut it and slice it any way you want. However, this rule, is hard to dispute. And keep in mind, once you have won or lost, you probably have eight to ten hours invested in each prospect. Quantify those Prime-Time hours – It will surprise you.

7 **Get Very Comfortable with Your BURTISMS.** You know them from the BAABCO App, yet they are worthless if you do not apply them. If you ask good engaging questions rather than tell, tell, tell, your prospect will feel much better about their engagement with you. Furthermore, when they trust you and witness your integrity, they generally do business with you. Sound good?

8 **Fire a Prospect.** Build to become confident at letting go. I'm speaking specifically to the prospect who continuously moves to next month time and time and time again. And too often, the longer the selling cycle, the less profitable the transaction. The Ten By Ten Strategy will be essential in weeding those folks off your Pipeline List. Let the competitors have them while you gain more time for Net New Prospecting with value buyers.

9 **Stay in front of your customers, suspects and prospects when you're not physically in front of them.** Build an email or LinkedIn list from every business card or intelligence you collect. Send out a personalized monthly newsletter that speaks more to an objective buyer beware approach, savings, efficiency, best practices for use and longevity of your industry products. Be the respected professional in your franchise. You will be amazed at how often your non-customers will unexpectedly ask you to come by and talk business. Microsoft Outlook, ZOHO, LinkedIn and Sales Force also have excellent software solutions to help you personalize your digital email and or video drip campaigns.

10 **Be Stralective.** Yes, I invented the word. Be strategic and selective of where you invest your time. Strategic is a plan. Selective refers to whom you go about strategically offering that plan to. It also helps to avoid just going through the motions. Being selective in your strategy almost always puts you in front of suspects who can truly value and benefit from your product or services.

11 **Befriend Your Competition.** Some of them sing like birds. It's amazing what they will share that can ultimately be applied in a future competitive situation. Just let them talk, talk, talk. Be a listening foe and keep your mouth shut. This is NOT about MUD SLINGING!!

12 **Take notes and listen.** I speak to this in the BAABCO App. You know the value of 70/30 listening. Intentionally keep it on your elevated awareness screen. Demonstrate to your suspect that you are listening. Listen and Silent have the same letters!

13 **Commit to an industry.** At least by your earliest thirties. Almost every industry has a lucrative sweet spot. I refer to positions that earn comfortable and multiple six-figure incomes, available to Sales Leaders. Outlast those that move on, and reap the benefits of what they left behind. Your industry seniority can provide you with extensive knowledge and respect from your suspects or clients compared to the newer person you might be competing with. In addition, keep yourself fresh and passionate.

14 **Read The Art of Professional Prospecting regularly or at least twice per year.** I created it as a guidebook for quick reference and completion. It will serve as a continuous reminder of the many strategies we discussed. I seriously request you review it semi-annually, apply your own Reality Points and study the Mental Workout Questions. You will be amazed at how your growth trends become very evident to you. Those trends will give you a sense of improved pride, monotony, or worse, disappointment. Either way, you must confront the person in the mirror and the Mental Workout Questions are designed for that sole purpose.

15 **Guard your energy and efforts.** After all, eight to ten hours are invested in many prospects . . . win or lose. Deploy early walk away strategies (especially in price wars) if you deem them counterproductive to your solid pipeline.

16 **Hire a personal part-time telemarketer or executive assistant.** Please see the BAABCO App for additional information.

17 **Lead your behavior with this thought: "If it is better for the customer, it costs more money."** This was one of the first lessons my father taught me. Start at manufacturer's suggested retail prices and always quantify your value first, before discounting.

18 **Accept this fact:** Out of the ten representatives you compete with in your territory, five will likely crash and burn within the first six to eighteen months, three will be middle-of-the-road competitors (win some, lose some mentalities) and two will be the top, most successful and feared Sales Leaders of all. Study, mirror the skill sets and commitment of the top two and you will be one of the top ten before you know it.

19 **If the account is worth going after, you have called twice and still have had no response, then show up in person.** Be prepared to identify and offer solutions for problems that have not been detected yet, versus those that already exist. This is a first step to being elevated to trusted advisor as opposed to merely one of many commodity sales reps.

20 **Finally, and most importantly, start your day with thirty to sixty minutes of quiet time with your God.** Study the word of your God. You will find courage, peace, comfort, joy, patience, integrity, leadership, appreciation, companionship, and the promise that your God wants only the best for you and yours.

MENTAL WORKOUT QUESTION:

Which are the Top Five that resonated most with you? How can you begin to implement those today?

1. _____

2. _____

3. _____

4. _____

5. _____

90 Trusted Advisor (Non-Evasive and Increased Evasive) Scripted Questions

When applying these questions, Varying Tonality, Phrasing, Physiology, Rapport and Strategic Timing are Critical to Your Success.

When Cold Calling:
- Would it be ok to ask for 30 seconds of your time to tell you why I dropped in or called?
- What have I said so far that caught your attention?
- In addition to you, who else should I speak with?

On building certainty as a trusted advisor with rapport:
- Thank you for seeing (talking with) me today, since last we spoke, has anything changed?
- Are you comfortable with me asking you questions about your budget, potential blind spots, current expenses, anything I deem vital to your business needs, equipment or point of need choices?
- What key things should I know about your business that will help me understand better/fully?
- Here is what I believe I know about your (company/industry)...am I accurate?

Getting to the next action steps:
- What are your expectations for today?
- In our earlier discussions you mentioned that xxxx was an issue...how long have you been dealing with that?
- Can you share with me what your biggest concern is/are with the present situation?
- How would you rate the present situation with (equipment/present vendor) bad, very bad, good or great?
- Can you tell me Why you rate it/them that way?

Prior to Presenting your solution/s:
- Are you excited to see our proposal?
- I'm excited to share our recommendations...are you?
- How would you feel today if our recommendations fulfilled or exceeded your needs/wants?
- Prior to starting, let's recap on what we have learned so far. Sound good?
- If our recommendations make sense for your business, can we move forward today?
- What will you need/want to see today in order to move forward?

- Before we get started, what are your expectations of me/us today?
- Before we start, can we agree on our next steps if we meet or exceed your expectations?
- Based on your expectations that we discussed, would you agree we hit the target?
- Are we headed in the right direction?
- So, what do you like so far?

Getting to the Pain:
- How serious is the problem right now and why?
- If the problem is not solved soon, what impact would that have on the business?
- What would you estimate the problem has cost the business in real dollars over the last (30,60,90 days / 6 months)?
- What would you say is the root of the problem...(equipment/vendor capacity-expertise)?
- Can you show me a good example?
- How do the other departments feel (impacted by) about this?
- Can you see how our solution is less costly than the current problem?
- What upsets you/them the most about the problem?
- Where do you want to see immediate improvement?
- Let me take a moment to summarize what I believe I heard so far...fair enough?

Budgeting/Expenses/Pricing:
- Who has ultimate decision authority on this type of operating expense?
- In addition to you, should anyone else be involved when reviewing the numbers?
- How should I make sure that everyone who should see these figures does see them?
- How long does the decision making on the financial part normally take?
- Have you/them decided if you/they will finance or pay cash?

On Timing:
- What is your time frame to execute on this matter?
- What are the reasons to execute at that time?
- When would you like to start seeing evidence of the benefits from our recommendations?
- How quickly might the issue get worse if action is not taken or procrastinated?

Avoiding Tangents:
- Can you tell me one more time about...?
- I want to be certain to not miss anything important, what is your next priority on the matter?
- We know this is important to you...do you mind if I take notes?
- Thank you for sharing...question, will anyone else be involved with you?
- How does your senior management feel about this and the timing to get it resolved?

Moving toward Closing the Sale:
- We have covered a lot...have we missed anything else on your mind or someone else's?
- Any aha moments yet on what we have covered today?
- If we are fortunate to earn your trust and move forward, what would your deciding factors have been to choose us?
- What would you think if I said, you can do it (better, faster) for less than you are now?
- Based on our solid recommendations, can you think of any reason to call anyone else?
- If you are planning to speak with anyone else, can you tell me why?
- Based on our discussions, I am certain you are a perfect fit for our proposal...ready to set up delivery for this week?
- The numbers hit the target of where you told me you wanted/needed to be. Ready to get this task from your desk to mine?
- Based on your situation, why is the current product/solution no longer acceptable?

Existing Account in Jeopardy:
- Have you caught us doing anything right?
- We did drop the ball. What can we do to get back in your good graces?
- Is there anyone else in addition to you that we should be doing damage control with?
- Aside from the frustration we caused, did the company/you lose money with us?
- On a scale of 1-10, how would you grade the value you have received for the money spent?

C-Level Strategy Questions:
- The new numbers, quantified over the next (3-5) years are significant, wouldn't you agree?
- Can you see how the solution we are recommending is less costly than the current problem?
- At what dollar threshold (cash or monthly investment) is your approval needed to move forward?
- Will your office support the preferred decision made by (Sally, Jim, Committee)?
- How much would you say the problem impacts the company P&L (daily, monthly, yearly)?
- How soon do you need the problem off your books?
- How do you think the company (morale, productivity, strategy) is impacted, once you execute?
- Is this a first order of business for you today (this week, month)?
- From your aerial view, what do you see as the cause of the problem?
- What prompted you to ask that question? What is the final buying criteria?

They want/need to think it over:
- Can you share what you will think over (cost, execution, onboarding) after this meeting?
- What is your process in thinking it over?
- I understand if you wish to think about it, have I answered all of your questions today?
- Is there anything important that I missed today?
- If I feel you are creating a costly delay, how do I convey that without offending you?
- Understood, if I do not hear back from you by (date), what is my next step?
- Is it that you really need to think it over or is it a no thank you?

When it is about Pricing or your ability to compete effectively as an expert/trusted advisor:
- Will the decision be based on price only, true cost or best value to the business?
- Can you give me a range of pricing you have received so far?
- Was the last decision based on price only, true cost or best value to the business?
- How did that strategy work for the business?
- Who are we being compared to?
- Does my competitor bring (Name your top 3 differentiators / your 4 corners)?
- Can we address our price difference and confirm if we really are higher based on true cost?
- If all prices were equal, could we receive your approval today to move forward?
- If we can meet you half way on the difference, can we move forward today?
- Do you or anyone at the company doubt our ability to fulfill the responsibility?
- Let's look at the numbers, bring it down to an hourly difference and compare (capacity, productivity, features) fair enough?
- Aside from pricing, what will we need to do differently in order to earn your trust?

Sales Preparation Checklist

Sales Leader Professional:

This valuable sales preparation list was gifted to me by one of my mentors. I have updated some of the relevant verbiage and now gift it to you. In addition, please be certain to download the **BAABCO Sales Development App** to further prepare you for your next in person or virtual sales call appointment!

On Preparing for Your next Sales Call...

Prior to, Did I:
- Research the client and opportunity prior to my call
- Learn something about the person and their business history prior to our meeting
- Forward a bulleted agenda to the client prior to our meeting
- Prepare three added values which are exclusive to our company
- Equip myself with the necessary tools and documents in preparation to Close
- Role Play in my mind or with my leader...goals, discovery components, next action steps

Introductions, Opening Statements, Rapport, Did I:
- Observe in person or virtually the prospect's office, décor, accolades, photos, commonalities
- Genuinely inquire about the prospect's personal interests, hobbies, family and so on
- Smoothly bridge to the topic of business
- Listen more than I spoke (70% listening-30% speaking / Silent has the same letters as Listen)
- Ask open questions about the prospect's one-to-five-year goals and beyond
- Ask the prospect what challenges & pain points they are facing and for how long
- Ask about the WHY, WHAT and HOW of their Value Proposition
- Ask the prospect about the challenges their industry and company may be facing

Qualifying, Did I:
- Ask what are their expectations from me and for our meeting
- Ask who in addition to them may be influencers or decision makers in the selection process
- Ask, IF we can meet or exceed their expectations, can we move forward today

- Ask if I could take notes and write them down during our meeting
- Ask what is their customary on boarding process for new vendors
- Ask how and why was the previous decision made (assuming you are displacing a competitor)
- Ask what they like about their present vendor & what would they specifically change
- Ask about their time frame, preferred financial method to implement and budget
- Ask is the decision to be made on price only, a hurry up mentality or overall best value
- Pinpoint specific needs that are a must for their upcoming implementation

Assessing, Did I:
- Incorporate my BURTISMS (open and close ended questions) Download the BAABCO app Now
- Ask about the enterprise structure (locations, private or publicly held)
- Ask the prospect about their company role & specifically their interests to the must haves
- Ask what risks or hurdles they may anticipate toward a successful implementation
- Ask how you and your company can provide help and solutions to solve the present challenges
- Ask how current trends may be impacting their business
- Ask WHAT IF questions...What IF we can, IF I meet your needs today, IF I - will You
- Ask what support they would like to see from me and my company post the implementation
- Ask about their short- & long-term goals, confirm our next actionable steps and schedule
- Ask and encourage the prospect to expand and elaborate (Tell me more) on their answers

Avoiding and Overcoming Objections or Stalls, Did I:
- Listen (Silent) to the entire objection or concern
- Listen to understand and not to respond (Covey)
- Pause for 3 seconds before responding, remain calm and not become defensive
- Address the objection or concern with an open-ended question
- Restate the prospect's objection or concern to be certain we agree (essential communication)
- Walk the prospect through the simplicity of requesting service from our company
- Fully address, answer and complete the six-step process to the objection or concern...

  Listen • Define • Rephrase • Isolate • Solve • Close or Next Actionable Step

In Person or Virtual Presentation, Did I:
- Prepare with all of the essential in person or virtual tools and best practices for success
- Prioritize the prospects stated needs – Do not waste your prospect's time if you have not
- Ask if anything has changed in the prospect's needs or wants since your last engagement
- Recreate the premise of their previous or current commitment
- Speak with and engage the prospect in layman's terms to the new benefits of your proposal
- Loop the specific benefits and build urgency to the present and future needs of the prospect
- Gain affirmation from the decision makers and or influencers before proceeding
- Demonstrate my professionalism, that of my company and steadily build genuine rapport
- Provide a summary of my product, service and solutions
- Focus on my prospect's needs, engage the prospect, build desire and ask for commitment

Closing, Did I:
- Affirm with my prospect their current challenges will be solved with my products and services
- Get my prospect to affirm my value proposition which my company, product and services will deliver to their needs
- Get my prospect to affirm the value and ask for their business... Can we move forward, Is there a reason we cannot move forward to day, Can we earn your authorization today...

Account Management, Did I:
- Write thank you notes or emails for meetings or their business (not during prime time)
- Ask for references and possible referrals
- Ask if they belong to a professional association where you can speak or present to members
- Establish cadence with the right company members to remain purposely visible, or send a thank you email to prospects which were lost to competition
- Ask for the most important things I can do in order to build upon a strong relationship

The 20 Daily Promising Practices

- They Build Trust, Urgency and Desire in order to shorten the selling cycle

- They are at 6 in the 11 steps of the Selling process as amateurs are at Step 2

- To be invited into the competitive arena, they prolong the Selling Process when it is to the Benefit and Value for the Prospect

- They self manage to the 20/30 Rule (5 move to next month/ 5 do nothing/ 5 are lost/ 5 are won) = 20 Closable Prospects every 30 Days

- Suspects are Identified and Valued over Prospects

- The Differentiating Actions between a Professional vs Amateur are Applied and the problems they solve are communicated before their professional title

- A Spoken Voice Mail is part of their Professional Communication

- Every Day is Treated as if it were the Last Day of the Month (A Valuable Lesson from Dad)

- FEAR does not prevent them from asking the Tough Questions. They apply the BURTISMS and Trusted Advisor Questions

- After a brief warm up, the QUALIFYING question is asked: Does Your Senior Management know We are Meeting Today?

- After a brief warm up, the PROBING question is asked: What are Your Expectations for Today?

- At the right moment, The QUANTIFYING question is asked: Will Your Decision be made on Price Only, True Cost or Overall Highest Value?

- They are Great at Quantifying the higher proposed costs down to actual Pennies and the long-term savings to significant Wind Falls.

- Expertise in the Top 5 to 7 products their company focuses growth on - is their lead in AND by Vertical Market

- They are GENUINE at communicating the Vision of Tomorrow's Value over Today's Price

- Continuous Sales Education, Self-Assessment and Reflection are part of their, Prize of the New Found Five Strategies

- They Stay the Course and Do Not Waver from their personal and Company Core Values.

- The Lion and Gazelle thought process (search QUOTE) is a part of their Strategic, Daily Motivation and Business Model

- The Company Value Proposition is applied Daily and Starts exclusively with their WHY, and then the What and How

- The Art of Professional Prospecting handbook and the Mental Workout Questions are studied and reflected upon at least twice per year

HOW DO YOU DEFINE SUCCESS?

The Ten By Ten Defined:

Ten Daily Net New Cold Calls between 8:30 - 10:00 AM

- Net New is anyone you have not spoken with in 90 Days.
- This includes your past, present, or never before done business with opportunities.

The 20/30 Rule Defined:

20 Closable Prospects Every 30 Days. Here's Why:

5 - Will move to next month despite the prospect's commitment to execute this month.

5 - Will do nothing at all...they decide to sell, merge, retire, re-evaluate, hold off, or lose interest for the moment.

5 - You will lose... timing, price, dynamics, solution, or product name. Remember, even the NFL and NBA Champions lost games during the season.

5 - You will win! Multiply your average transaction size X 5, and you are likely at or above your monthly quota! Nice Job!

BAABCO Leadership Consulting

BAABCO Leadership Consulting brings awareness and intentionality to these important professional development sessions through:

- The Pentagon Leadership Series which focuses on Accountability, Effectiveness, Mentoring, Communication, Influence and Loyalty

- Creation and Implementation of Your Organization Value Proposition

- All Levels of Customer and Employee Engagement

- Creation and Implementation of Your Organization Core Values

- New Business Development via the Art of Professional Prospecting Handbook, the BAABCO Sales Training and Development App, Role Play Scenarios, and certification of the Paul Martinelli Sales Mastermind Curriculum.

- Leadership to Grow Leaders, One on One Coaching, Essential Dialogues, Leadership Moments and Communication Protocol

- The John Maxwell Leadership Development principles brought to You via the Certified Coaching Accreditation Sessions and DISC Personality Assessments

Leader, please visit us today at www.BAABCO.biz for a more comprehensive view of our distinctive BAABCO, John Maxwell and Paul Martinelli Professional Development services.

BAABCO
Leadership Consulting

About the Author

Burt grew up in the Chicago and north suburbs area. Dad was a successful insurance sales executive and mom was a domestic engineer, raising the 4 children.

After working for his dad during summer breaks, he attended college for a couple of years before entering the restaurant industry. He was promoted quickly and oversaw locations in Illinois, Arkansas and Texas. It was during those years that he learned the necessary skill sets to lead and motivate multiple contributing teams while operating in the black.

In his strategic vision and heart, Burt's ultimate goal was to follow in Dad's foot steps. This was because nothing compared to the excitement of truly owning your income growth potential, building lasting friendships and delivering essential customer value, as he witnessed with his Dad's business.

The transition to a highly successful career in professional sales began in the copier industry for 12 years followed by 28 years with the global leader of technology financing serving dealer and manufacturer distributors. An unending commitment to daily Prospecting, Purposeful Visibility for his clients and a full understanding of his Value Proposition drove then and continues today, to fuel his success. For Burt, It is always about catching the competition asleep at the wheel and crossing the finish line at 250 MPH!!

Burt now devotes his time to the esteemed clients of BAABCO Leadership Consulting, Sales Training and Development, BAABCO Properties, family and traveling with his wife of 33 years, Dr. Alicia Villarreal.

www.ingramcontent.com/pod-product-compliance
Lightning Source LLC
Chambersburg PA
CBHW042122190326
41519CB00031B/7582